HIPPOS

By Melissa Cole
Photographs by Tom and Pat Leeson

BLACKBIRCH®
PRESS

THOMSON
★
GALE

San Diego • Detroit • New York • San Francisco • Cleveland • New Haven, Conn. • Waterville, Maine • London • Munich

THOMSON

GALE

JAN 1 6 2003

Photo Credits: Cover © PhotoDisc; all photos © Tom and Pat Leeson Nature Wildlife Photography; back cover, page 3 © CORBIS; page 9 © Gary Vestal/Leeson Photo

LIBRARY OF CONGRESS CATALOGING-IN-PUBLICATION DATA

Cole, Melissa S.
 Hippos / by Melissa S. Cole.
  p. cm. — (Wild Africa series)
Summary: Examines the life of the hippopotamus, pointing out differences between the two remaining species and the impact humans have had, and continue to have, on these African mammals.
 ISBN 1-56711-635-3 (hardback : alk. paper)
 1. Hippopotamidae—Juvenile literature. [1. Hippopotamus. 2. Endangered species.] I. Title.
 QL737.U57 C66 2003
 599.63'5—dc21   2002004232

Printed in China
10 9 8 7 6 5 4 3 2 1

Contents

Introduction

Hippopotamuses belong to a group of animals called Artiodactyla. This group of animals also includes pigs, deer, and camels. Ancient Greeks gave the hippopotamus its name, which means "river horse."

Today, there are two hippo species: the river, or common, hippo and the pygmy hippo. Until recently, common hippos ranged throughout most of Africa. Hunting and other human activities have reduced hippo populations. Today, there

The name *hippopotamus* means "river horse."

are only about 15,000 common hippos living in the wild. Most common hippos live in the African countries of Zaire, Zambia, Malawi, Mozambique, and Zimbabwe. Common hippos live mostly beside rivers and lakes, and on the grassy savannas.

Pygmy hippos are more rare than common hippos. There are only about 2,000 pygmy hippos left in the wild. These animals live in the western African countries of Liberia, Ivory Coast, and Sierra Leone. They prefer to live in swampy areas deep within thick forests.

Hippos spend most of their time in or near the water.

The Hippo's Body

The common hippo's body is huge, muscular, and barrel-shaped. It is the third-largest land mammal on earth—only rhinos and elephants are larger. Common hippos are about 5 feet (1.5 m) tall and 11 feet (3.4 m) long. A full-grown hippo weighs around 5,000 pounds (2,268 kg), though some grow to be more than 7,000 pounds (3,175 kg). Male hippos, or bulls, are usually larger than female hippos, or cows.

Pygmy hippos weigh about 400 pounds (1,864 kg), stand between 30 and 39 inches (76 to 99 cm) tall, and are about 5 feet (1.5 m) long. Their small

The body of a hippo is barrel-shaped and very muscular.

heads and long necks give their bodies a bullet-like shape.

Common hippos have thick, stubby legs and large round feet. The feet of common hippos and pygmy hippos are different because common hippos spend a lot of time in the water and pygmy hippos do not. Common hippos have 4 toes on each foot, with stretchy, web-like skin in between each toe. When a hippo spreads its toes apart, the webbing expands. The hippo can then use its feet as flippers to help it swim.

Pygmy hippos do not have webbing in between their toes, but their toes spread out more than a common hippo's. This helps the pygmy hippo keep its balance on the uneven floor of the forest.

Hippos have short, wide legs and 4 toes on each foot.

A hippo can close its nostrils when underwater and open them to breathe above water.

A common hippo's eyes, nose, and ears are on top of its head. That allows the hippo to see, breathe, and hear by rising only a few inches out of the water. When hippos dive into the water, they fold their ears tightly against the sides of their heads. Their nostrils clamp shut to keep water from entering their lungs.

Adult hippos can stay underwater for more than 5 minutes. Hippos can move along the bottom of a riverbed by pushing off the bottom with their rear legs and landing on their front legs.

Hippos are an important part of the ecosystem. Their dung feeds tiny plants and animals that live in the water. As hippos move along the bottom of a river, they stir up creatures that are eaten by large fish. Catfish and sucker fish keep hippos clean by nibbling algae and dead skin from their hides. Hippos even let these "cleaner fish" swim into their mouths to pick food from their teeth. On the surface, birds—such as cattle egrets and oxpeckers—help clean a hippo's skin by picking off insects.

Adult hippos can stay underwater for more than 5 minutes.

Special Features

Hippos have thick skin to protect them from predators such as crocodiles, hyenas, and lions. A common hippo's skin is grayish-brown on its back, and pinkish on its belly. Pygmy hippos are darker in color, with a yellowish underbelly. Hippos have hair on their snouts, the tips of their ears, and on their tails.

Even though hippo skin is thick, it is sensitive. Hippos often roll in mud to coat and protect their skin from insects and sunburn. Common hippos have special red oil that comes out of their skin. People once thought that these animals were sweating blood. In fact, this thick, red liquid helps keep the hippo's skin moist. It also kills germs and can heal wounds. In pygmy hippos, this oil is clear.

Rolling in mud covers a hippo's skin for protection.

Hippos have very good hearing.

Scientists do not think hippos have sharp eyesight, but they are able to see in the dark. They rely on their sense of smell instead of their vision to sense predators, and to find their way home after feeding.

Hippos have very good hearing, both above and below water. Hippos have a special way of hearing underwater sounds. Sound waves enter through a hippo's jaw. The sound waves then travel into the hippo's lower ear. If the sound is louder in the left ear than in the right, the hippo knows that the sound came from the left side.

Social Life

Common hippos are social animals that often form groups of more than 20. These groups—called crèches—are mostly made up of cows, calves, and teenage hippos. One dominant, or lead, bull protects a crèche.

During the day, cows and calves stay in the water. There they keep cool, take naps, wallow in the mud, and groom one another with their teeth. The dominant bull establishes his territory along the riverbank beside the crèche.

Hippos like to live in groups.

Bull hippos mark their territories with droppings, both in and out of the water. They rapidly flap their tails to scatter dung for several yards. Other hippos smell the bull's scent and know that the territory is taken.

A bull may hold the same territory for a few months or for several years. Individual territories can measure 1,000 feet (305 m) long and more than 165 feet (50 m) wide. Sometimes two bulls challenge each other on the border of their territories. They rush at each other with their mouths wide open and meet jaw-to-jaw.

If one hippo tries to take over the territory of another, they fight in a different way. The two animals stand side by side and face in opposite directions.

When two bulls challenge each other, they rush at each other with mouths open wide.

Then they swing their heads sideways and try to drive their sharp tusks, or teeth, into the other's rump and sides. The fight continues until one animal retreats. A fight may last more than an hour!

Pygmy hippos prefer to live alone or in groups of two or three. Zookeepers have found that pygmy hippos grow ill tempered if they are forced to be close to more than a few other hippos at once. Both male and female pygmy hippos establish territories, which they mark with piles of dung.

Hippos use sounds to communicate. These sounds range from deep, rumbling grunts to high-pitched squeaks. Scientists have also heard hippos make clicking and whistling sounds similar to those made by whales and dolphins.

Hippos can make sounds above and below the water at the same time! They do this by humming through their mouths and nostrils. Underwater sounds start in their larynx, or voice box, and travel through their throats and into the water. The sound travels through the water and can be heard on the surface as well.

Hippos use sounds to communicate—above and below the water.

Feeding

Hippos are herbivores, or plant eaters. They can eat over 100 pounds (45 kg) of vegetation a day. Their main food is grass. They also eat shoots, leaves, fallen fruit, and water plants.

Although hippos are not nocturnal (active at night instead of during the day), they feed at night when temperatures are cooler. Cows with calves feed together, while male hippos generally feed alone. Hippos spend much of the night grazing, and stop only occasionally to lie down for a nap.

Hippos are herbivores, which means they are plant eaters.

Hippos follow well-worn paths to feeding areas, and eat grass as they go along. They may wander from 3 to 6 miles (5 to 10 km) within their feeding grounds each night. When the sun rises, hippos go back to their water holes to rest, socialize, and digest their food.

Hippos have between 38 and 44 teeth. Their wide, ridged molars grind up grass before they swallow it. Grass is stringy and hard to digest, so hippos produce a lot of dung. They scatter droppings along trails. This helps them find their way between their feeding ground and water hole.

Hippos have wide, flat teeth that grind up grass.

The Mating Game

Both common and pygmy cows are usually ready to mate when they are 3 or 4 years old. Males are able to mate when they are 5 years old, but they usually do not get a chance until they are a few years older. They need time to establish their territory near a crèche. Cows do not wander far from the crèche, so the strongest bulls stake their territories as close to the crèche as they can. This gives them the best chance to mate. Younger, weaker bulls are forced to live farther away from the crèche, so they are not as likely to find a mate.

Females attract males by making a huffing, snorting sound. Mating occurs in shallow water, usually near dusk. After mating, the pair separates.

The strongest bulls have the best chance of mating with females.

Common hippos often mate in February and August. Calves are born 8 months later during one of two rainy seasons. This timing helps the calves survive because there is plenty of food during the rainy season. A mother must eat a lot to be able to produce enough milk for her calf.

A young calf swims with its mother.

Raising Young

A hippo's gestation period, or pregnancy, lasts from 7 to 8 months. When a cow is ready to give birth, she moves away from the group. She will often give birth in water. Seconds after the calf is born, the mother hippo pushes it to the surface of the water to breathe. Newborn calves weigh between 50 to 100 pounds (23 to 45 kg), and are about 3 feet (91.4 cm) long and 2 feet (60.06 cm)

A newborn hippo is pushed to the surface of the water to breathe.

tall. Pygmy calves are tiny. They weigh between 6 and 14 pounds (2.7 to 6.4 kg) and are only 1 foot long (30.5 cm). Within a few minutes, calves are able to walk. After an hour, the hungry newborn begins to nurse.

During their first months of life, calves quickly gain weight on their diet of rich hippo milk. Hippo calves can nurse on land and underwater. Calves must hold their breath while they nurse, so they frequently surface for air. When calves are 4 months old, they begin to eat grass and water plants. By the time they are 8 months old, they eat only plants.

In the water, a newborn often rides on its mother's back. As the baby grows, it learns to swim beside its mother. For the first few weeks, common hippo mothers and their calves separate themselves from the group. Later, they join the rest of the crèche, where calves play together and learn important social skills.

Mother hippos often leave the crèche to feed or to roll in the mud. Cows take turns protecting the group of baby hippos within the crèche. One or two mothers always stay near the calves to keep an eye out for predators. Watchful mothers also keep a lookout for ill-tempered bulls that might mistakenly crush a calf. Females allow well-behaved males into the crèche, but if bulls become noisy, they are chased away.

Mother hippos are strict with their babies to help keep them safe.

Although cows are very affectionate with their young, mother hippos can be strict if their babies do not behave. When a calf does not stay close to its mother, she nudges it with her head. She may even nip her calf or swing her head against it and knock it down.

Female calves stay close to their mothers until they are about 4 years old. Even after a female calf is too old to be fed and cared for by its mother, it remains with the crèche it was born into. Male hippos often leave their mothers when they are one year old. At this age, young bulls go off to fight with other males to gain territories of their own.

Hippos and Humans

Throughout history, humans have hunted hippos for sport, meat, and ivory. Hippo meat is a food source for many African people. Hippo hides are used for clothing and blankets. Because an international law bans the buying and selling of elephant ivory, many poachers (illegal hunters) have turned to hunting hippos for their ivory teeth.

Growing human populations have forced hippos and humans to live closer together as humans take over hippo habitats. Hippos can get used to being

Hippo populations are threatened by hunting and the growth of towns and villages.

around people and become unafraid of them. When this happens, hippos may raid agricultural crops and cause damage to property. Hippos that are not afraid of humans can be dangerous, and people sometimes shoot them.

In Liberia, pygmy hippos are losing their habitats because people are cutting down forests for wood and farmland. If these areas are not protected, the pygmy hippo could face extinction.

Many people are working hard to protect hippos. Tourists will pay to see hippos in the wild, so many local Africans work as guides and park rangers instead of as poachers. The African government is trying to set aside more land for wildlife parks, where hippos may live for many years to come.

Hippo Facts

Scientific Name: Artiodactyla
Shoulder Height: 5 ft. (1.5 m)
Body Length: 11 ft. (3.4 m)
Weight: 5,000–7,000 pounds (2,268–3,175 kg)
Color: grayish-brown
Reaches sexual maturity at: 3–4 years old
Gestation (pregnancy period): 8 months
Litter Size: one calf
Favorite Food: grass
Range: African savannas

Glossary

Crèche A nursery group made up of mother hippos and their calves.

Gestation period The length of time during which a female hippo is pregnant.

Herbivores Animals that only eat plants.

Poach To illegally hunt an animal.

Territory An area, or home range, where an animal spends most of its time.

Further Reading

Books

Walker, Sally M. *Hippos.* Minneapolis: CarolRhoda Publishing, 1997.

Johnson, Marianne. *Hippos.* New York: Powerkids Press, 1997.

Markert, Jenny. *Hippos.* Minneapolis: Child's World, 2001.

Web sites

Zambia National Tourist Board: Hippopotamus Page

http://www.zambiatourism.com/travel/Wildlife/hippo.htm

Creature World: Hippopotamus Page

http://www.pbs.org/kratts/world/africa/hippo/

San Antonio Zoo: Hippopotamus Page

http://www.sazoo-aq.org/hippo.html

Index